Where's SANTA?

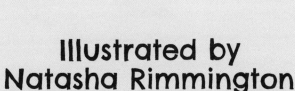
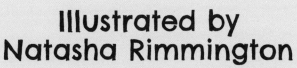

Illustrated by
Natasha Rimmington

ARCTURUS

ARCTURUS

This edition published in 2022 by Arcturus Publishing Limited
26/27 Bickels Yard, 151–153 Bermondsey Street,
London SE1 3HA

Author: William Potter
Illustrator: Natasha Rimmington
Editor: Violet Peto
Designer: Amy McSimpson
Design Manager: Jessica Holliland
Managing Editor: Joe Harris

ISBN: 978-1-3988-1101-0
CH010097NT
Supplier 29, Date 0622, Print run 11800

Printed in China

Ho ho ho!
Are you ready to come
on a search-and-find
adventure?

Sleigh Bells Are Ringing!

December is a very busy time for Santa. He has to gather and deliver presents as well as check out who's been naughty and who's been good! Join him as he races around the globe making his Christmas deliveries. Can you find him in each location? There are extra items to search for, too, as clumsy Claus has dropped a few stocking fillers along the way! Help him find all the missing gifts and finish his delivery in time for Christmas.

The International Elf Service

requests the assistance of _____

to help Santa find his way around the world.

So jump on Santa's sleigh and set off on a magical journey with our festive friend. You'll see many wonders along the way, from magical beasts and fantastic feasts to snowy scenes and candy kingdoms.
Can you find Santa in each location?

Once you spot him, stay a while longer to explore the local delights. Maybe you'll see something to add to your Christmas list!

What are you waiting for?
Your sleigh awaits!

Sliding Santa

Living at the North Pole, Santa is used to dashing around on skates and sleighs. Can you find him hiding on the ice?

Have you spotted us?

Under the Lights of Norway

Santa has arrived in Norway to find new reindeer to pull his sleigh. Can you see him in the snowy scene?

Up in the Air

This bright balloon festival is causing a traffic jam in the sky.
Can you spot Santa's sleigh high in the clouds?

Have you spotted us?

Chilly Check-In

You have to wrap up warm to stay at this ice hotel in Sweden. Even Santa feels a chill. Can you spy him?

Have you spotted us?

What a Performance!

Roll up for a sensational circus! Santa can't resist a little clowning around, but he might not have chosen the best place to hide. Where is he?

Have you spotted us?

13

Curtain Call

The Nutcracker is a traditional Christmas ballet, and Santa wouldn't miss a chance to watch it. But where is he in the opera house?

Have you spotted us?

15

Fantasy Kingdom

The temperature is rising as we arrive in Lava Land. Even wizards, goblins, and dragons celebrate Christmas! Has Santa paid a visit?

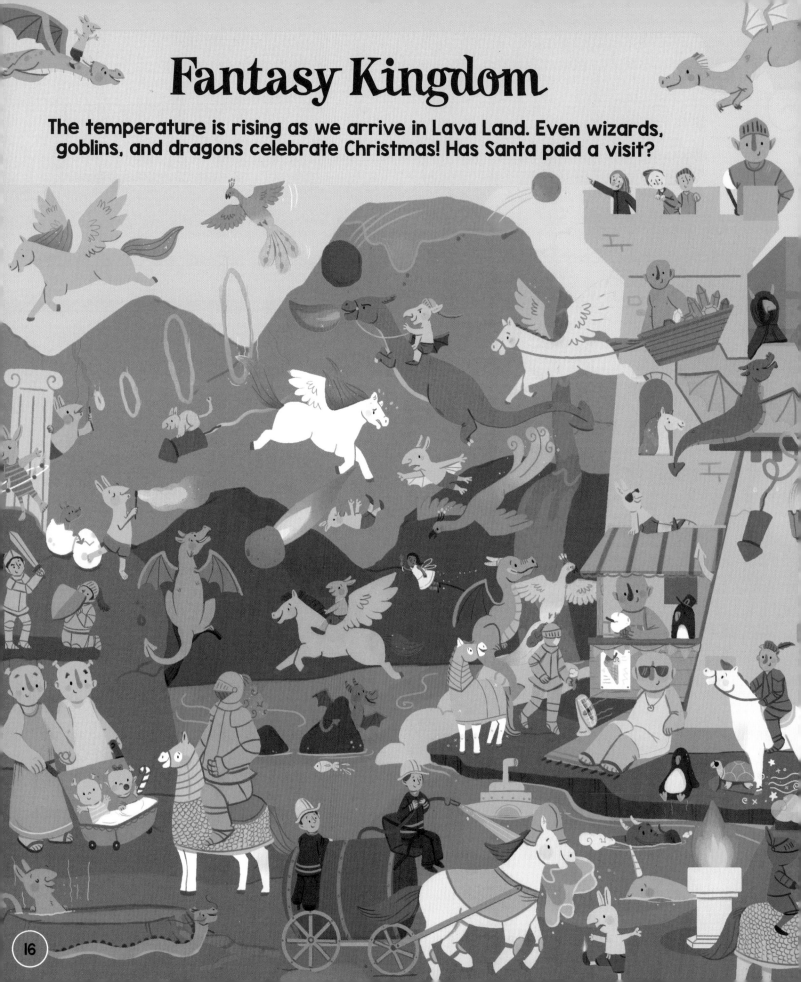

Have you spotted us?

Get Your Skates On!

It's winter in Moscow, and there are many festive treats on offer around the ice rink. Try not to slip over as you seek Santa!

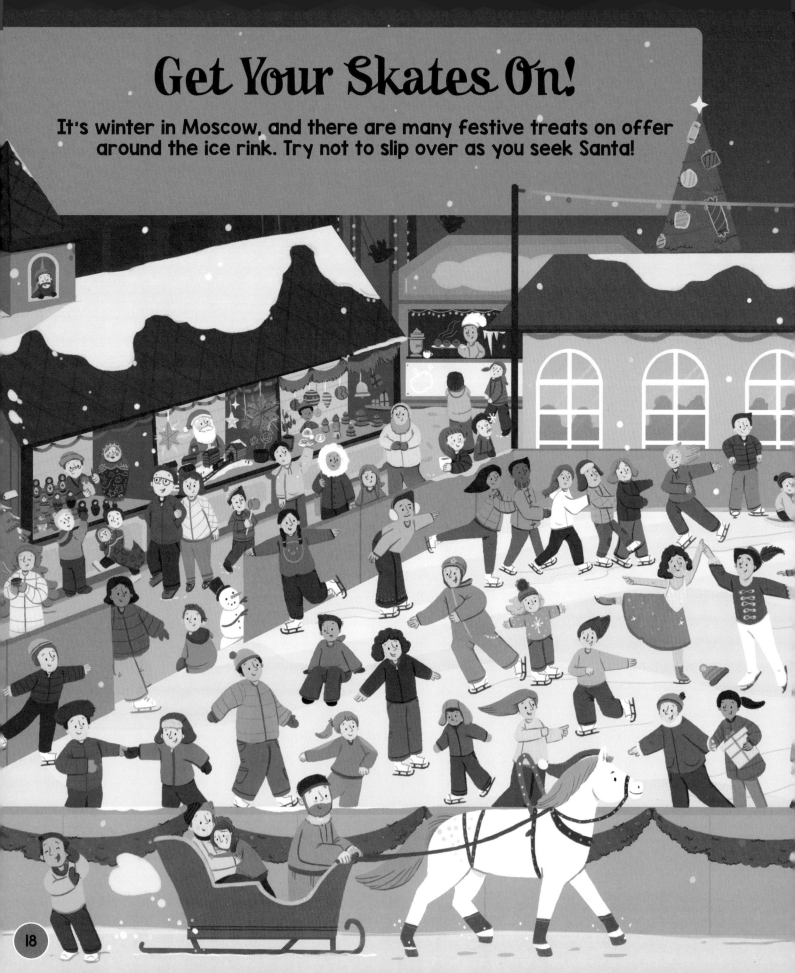

Have you spotted us?

19

Partying in Transylvania

Not only is it Christmas, but it is also Dracula's 276th birthday! Santa has been invited to a fang-tastic ball to celebrate. He can't wait to tuck into the enormous cake. Can you spot him?

Have you spotted us?

21

Wild in the Woods

Climbing, swinging, sliding, and leaping ... this outdoor adventure playground has lots to offer. Where's Santa and what activity should he join in?

Get in Shape

With Christmas coming, Santa needs to be in good shape for the big day. Can you spot him working out in the gym?

Have you spotted us?

25

Chugging Along

If Santa ever wanted to swap his sleigh for a boat, what better place to go than the canals of Amsterdam? Can you spot him among the tall, bright buildings?

Left or Right?

Santa's found himself in an amazing maze. It looks like lots of fun, but will he find his way out in time for Christmas?

Have you spotted us?

Irish Jig

There's always a friendly welcome in Ireland, and plenty of dancing. Can you spy Santa shaking a leg?

Have you spotted us?

Folklore Friends

Santa's elves have invited him to meet other fairy folk. In a land of giants and gnomes, you'll need to look high and low for Mr. Claus.

Ski Dream

It's busy on the slopes. Can you dodge the polar bears
and find Santa and his sleigh?

Have you spotted us?

Fairground Fun

Bumper cars! The big wheel! The ghost train! With all the fun at the fair, which ride will Santa Claus choose?

BUMPER CARS

Fashion Parade

Maybe Santa would like a change from his red and white suit.
Can you spot him in the trendy crowd at this Paris fashion show?

Have you spotted us?

Buon Appetito!

It's time for a spot of lunch, and where better to feast than Italy? Where has Santa chosen to eat today?

Have you spotted us?

41

Chocolate Cheer

A lot of children have asked for chocolate for Christmas, so Santa has to check supplies—and have a taste! Can you spy him lending a helping hand in the chocolate factory?

Magical Mine

It's hard work digging for gems. When Santa pays a visit to the Crystal Caves, even he has to join in. Can you spot him in the tunnels?

Have you spotted us?

45

Skateboarder Santa

Who asked for a skateboard for Christmas? It's on its way once Santa has checked that it's safe. Can you spot him?

Have you spotted us?

47

Witchy World

Santa's has come to Witchville to buy flying dust for his reindeer.
He's left his sleigh behind, so how did he fly here?

Have you spotted us?

Dentist

Magic Tree

Hubble Bubble
Tea Rooms

Potion Store

Fortune
Telling

SCHOOL BUS

Wands &
Beyond

49

Santa Pamper

Before he greets children in December, Santa wants to
look his best, so he's gone to the salon for a beard trim.
Doesn't he look dashing?

Have you spotted us?

Arabian Adventure

Magic sleigh or magic carpet—which is the best way to get around?
Can you spy Santa in the busy bazaar?

Safari Santa

Santa's on safari bringing Christmas to the animals in Kenya.
One of the elephants received a basketball. Now, where is Santa?

Have you spotted us?

Monster Drive-In

It's movie night in Germany's spooky Black Forest. Santa is enjoying a slime potion refreshment. Go say boo to him!

Have you spotted us?

Fantastic Fruit

Mrs. Claus asked Santa to buy some fruit on his journey. There's so much choice at this market in Nigeria, he doesn't know where to start. Show Santa around.

Have you spotted us?

Muddled in Mumbai

Shopping for spice in India, Santa has lost his way in the busy streets of Mumbai. Where is he now?

Have you spotted us?

61

Under the Moonlight

With a full moon in the sky, everyone's gathered for a beach party here in Thailand. Even Santa has slipped on his swimwear. Can you see him?

Sweet Streets

Candy Land is the sweetest spot for a visit. Santa has dropped in to collect cookies for his reindeer but can't resist playing a game first.

Have you spotted us?

Fantasy Feast

The blossoms are blooming in this Japanese garden. It's perfect for a picnic, with animals and magical creatures all invited. Santa, too! Offer him some sushi!

Have you spotted us?

Beach BBQ

It's summer in Australia at Christmas. Spot Santa enjoying the sun, surf, scuba, and a beach-side barbecue Down Under.

Have you spotted us?

Temple Trek

This jungle temple has been lost for centuries. Of course, Santa knew about it—he knows everyone's address! Where is he hiding?

Peak Viewing

Here in the mountains of Peru, Santa is looking for a toy llama to add to his sack. Can you find our festive friend?

WE DID IT!
Young Climbers Club

Have you spotted us?

73

Fairy-Tale Festival

All the magical folk have gathered for one huge party,
with games, food, and dancing. Was Santa invited?
See if you can find out.

Have you spotted us?

Jungle Japes

Santa has trekked through the Amazon rain forest
to deliver presents to all the children that live there.
Can you spot him in the undergrowth?

Have you spotted us?

Coast with the Most

On this glitzy Miami beachside, photographers are taking snaps of a superstar. But, who could be more famous than Santa? Can you get a picture of him?

Have you spotted us?

Moviemakers

Cast and crew are busy making movies at the Hollywood studios. Look! Is that Santa or an actor playing him?

Have you spotted us?

Cowboy Central

Feeling hungry, Santa has stopped off at a Texas hoedown for a burger. Lead him to the barbecue before he gets roped in for the line dancing!

Have you spotted us?

Totally Trucks

Santa has many toy trucks to deliver this year. He has come to the monster truck arena for research. Can you find him trying his best to be heard over the engine noise?

Santa Cruise

Christmas is over. Now Santa can take a well-earned break.
Spot him taking it easy on this cruise.

Sea Sleigh

Have you spotted us?

Which silhouette exactly matches Santa and his sleigh?

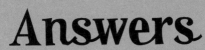
Answers

Pages 4-5 Sliding Santa

Pages 6-7 Under the Lights of Norway

Pages 8-9 Up in the Air

Pages 10-11 Chilly Check-In

Pages 12-13 What a Performance!

Pages 14-15 Curtain Call

Pages 16–17 Fantasy Kingdom

Pages 18–19 Get Your Skates On!

Pages 20–21 Partying in Transylvania

Pages 22–23 Wild in the Woods

Pages 24–25 Get in Shape

Pages 26–27 Chugging Along

Pages 28-29 Left or Right?

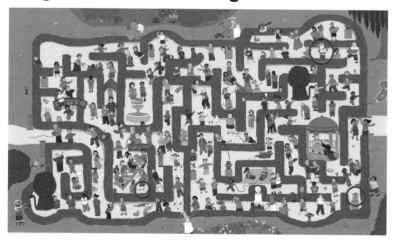

Pages 30-31 Irish Jig

Pages 32-33 Folklore Friends

Pages 34-35 Ski Dream

Pages 36-37 Fairground Fun

Pages 38-39 Fashion Parade

Pages 40-41 Buon Appetito!

Pages 42-43 Chocolate Cheer

Pages 44-45 Magical Mine

Pages 46-47 Skateboarder Santa

Pages 48-49 Witchy World

Pages 50-51 Santa Pamper

Pages 52–53 Arabian Adventure

Pages 54–55 Safari Santa

Pages 56–57 Monster Drive-In

Pages 58–59 Fantastic Fruit

Pages 60–61 Muddled in Mumbai

Pages 62–63 Under the Moonlight

Pages 64–65 Sweet Streets

Page 66–67 Fantasy Feast

Pages 68–69 Beach BBQ

Pages 70–71 Temple Trek

Page 72–73 Peak Viewing

Page 74–75 Fairy-Tale Festival

Page 76-77 Jungle Japes

Page 78-79 Coast with the Most

Pages 80-81 Moviemakers

Page 82-83 Cowboy Central

Page 84-85 Totally Trucks

Page 86-87 Santa Cruise

Page 88 Answer: C